# ALEXANDER
# HAMILTON
## COLORING BOOK

Steven James Petruccio

Dover Publications, Inc.
Mineola, New York

## NOTE

Follow a timeline of Alexander Hamilton's life and you'll soon know why he remains such a well-known figure in American history. Along with being an important pioneer in the early formation of the nation's government, he also led troops in battles against the British, established The Bank of New York, founded the *New-York Evening Post*, and served as the first Secretary of the Treasury. Enjoy learning even more about this Founding Father as you add color to the detailed illustrations provided in this coloring book.

*Bibliographical Note*

*Alexander Hamilton Coloring Book* is a new work, first published by Dover Publications, Inc., in 2017.

*International Standard Book Number*

*ISBN-13: 978-0-486-81212-0*
*ISBN-10: 0-486-81212-X*

Manufactured in the United States by LSC Communications
81212X02    2017
www.doverpublications.com

Hamilton was born on the Caribbean island of Nevis in 1757 (although some experts contend the year was 1755). He did not attend the local Christian school, but became an avid reader.

At the age of ten his family moved to St. Croix, and young Hamilton began working for the Beekman & Cruger trading company. After he spent a few years acquiring a mastery of international currency, he was trusted enough to be placed in charge of the company while the owner was at sea.

In 1772 a terrible hurricane hit St. Croix. Hamilton penned a descriptive letter about the event, and the letter was published and read by local merchants.

# Write A Letter

ACTIVITY: Use a pen, pencil, or make your own quill pen (see page 15 for instructions), and write a letter, poem, or rap to describe an important event in your own life.

In 1773 Hamilton was sent to the American colonies to be educated, funded by local merchants who were impressed by his letter. During the voyage, the ship encountered a storm and Hamilton helped by bailing out seawater and putting out fires on board.

He acquired a tutor at Elizabethtown Academy in New Jersey.
As a student, Hamilton had a single-minded focus on his work
and was often observed studying until midnight.

In 1774 Hamilton wrote his first political pamphlet, *A Full Vindication of the Measures of the Congress*, under the pseudonym of *A Friend to America*, urging colonists to rally around Congress.

Hamilton spoke to an angry mob gathered at King's College (now Columbia University) looking for the school's loyalist president, Myles Cooper. Hamilton's lengthy speech helped Cooper escape to safety.

In 1775 Hamilton joined the New York militia—later called *The Hearts of Oak*—and organized fellow members/students on a raid to steal British artillery. He was appointed a captain with command of the New York Provincial Company of Artillery in March, 1776.

Hamilton was in attendance as the Declaration of Independence was read to George Washington's troops in New York on July 9, 1776.

# Create A Colonial Quill Pen

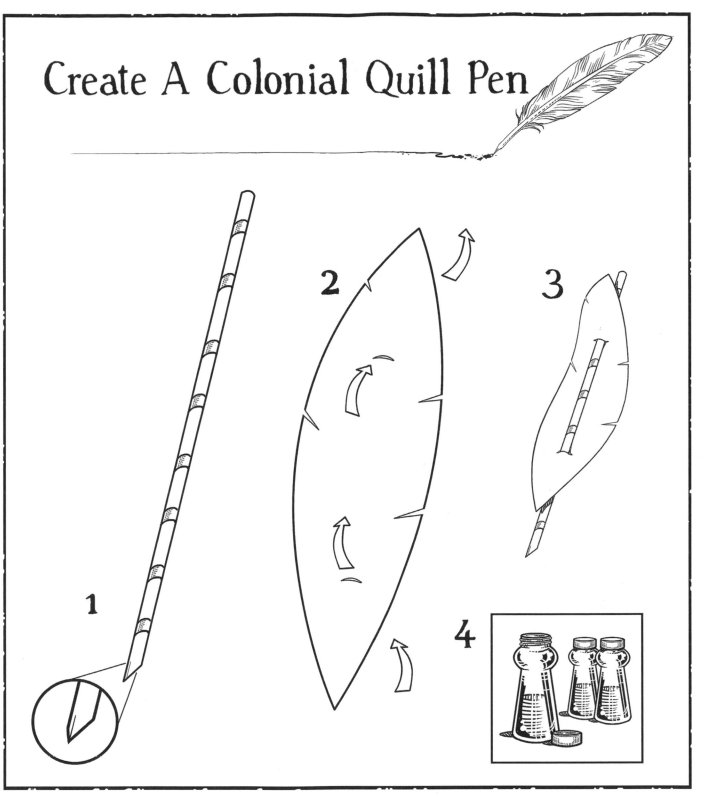

1  Use a standard 7" plastic drinking straw and cut the tip on an angle, then cut a small slit in the center of the tip.

2  Use a 6" piece of construction paper and cut out an almond shape, then cut 2 small slits across the center.

3  Weave the straw through the paper.

4  Use food coloring as "ink", dip the tip of the pen in, and write!

On January 3, 1777, Hamilton led his troops in The Battle of Princeton, using cannons to blast Nassau Hall. It is said that a hole was blasted right through a portrait of King George II that was hanging on a wall inside!

On March 1, 1777, Hamilton was appointed as *aide-de-camp* to General Washington. He would serve in this role through 1781.

During this time Hamilton began a correspondence with
Elizabeth Schuyler of Albany, whom he would later marry.

In 1781 Hamilton led the assault on Redoubt No. 10 at Yorktown, the last major battle of the Revolutionary War.

ACTIVITY: Draw a portrait of your favorite patriot.

# Make a Tricorn Hat

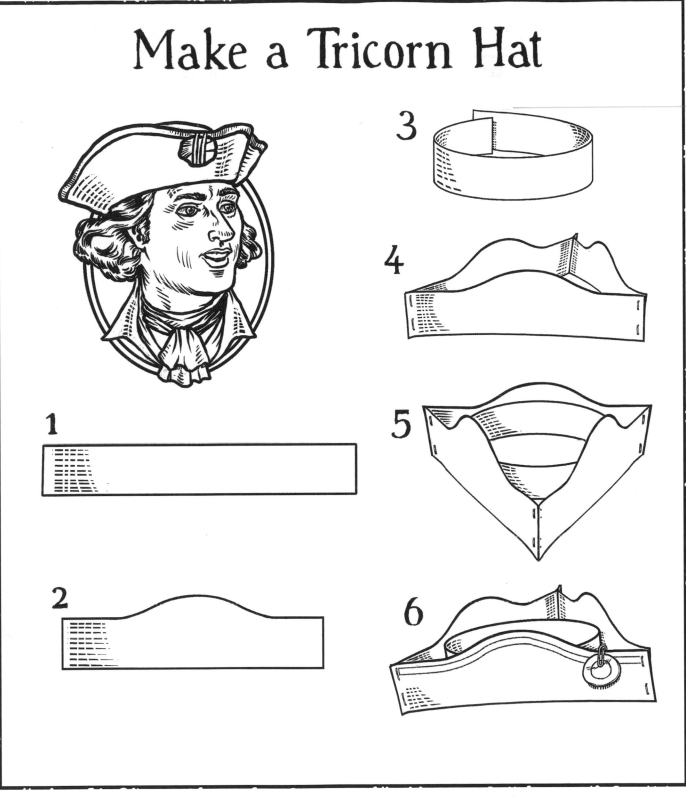

1. Cut a 4" wide strip of paper long enough to fit around your head, about 12" – 18".
2. Cut 3 strips of 14" long paper, 5" high curving to 6" high at center.
3. Wrap strip 1 around your head to form a headband and tape it in place.
4. Staple the 3 strips together at the edges to form a triangle shape.
5. Place the triangle over the circle headband and glue the center of each together.
6. Decorate the hat with circle or square insignia and paperclip it to the edge.

In 1782 Hamilton returned to New York and became a lawyer after just six months of study. In 1783 he established a legal practice in his home. He defended loyalists, feeling that the nation should adopt a policy of "forgive and forget."

Hamilton established The Bank of New York in 1784, making it the second-oldest bank in the United States behind the Bank of North America.

Hamilton served as a New York delegate to the Constitutional Convention of 1787, where he strongly supported the idea of separation of power between the individual states and the federal government.

Hamilton wrote most of a series of essays, along with James Madison and John Jay, under the pseudonym "Publius", from 1787 to 1788. These essays are now collectively known as *The Federalist Papers*, and promoted the ratification of the new Constitution.

In 1789 George Washington was sworn in as the *first* President of the United States. Hamilton and Thomas Jefferson were among his *first* cabinet members.

In September of 1789 Hamilton was appointed as the first Secretary of the Treasury. In this role he would establish a plan for our monetary system.

# Create Your

ACTIVITY: Alexander Hamilton and Benjamin Franklin are among only a few people to appear on U.S. currency who were not U.S. presidents. Throughout the nation's history, Hamilton's image has appeared on more currency than anyone else. Design your own U.S. currency.

# Own Currency

In 1790 Hamilton met with Thomas Jefferson and James Madison to resolve the U.S. debt issue. Part of this "Dinner Table Bargain" included moving the nation's capital to what would become Washington, D.C.

Federalist

Democratic-Republican

Hamilton established a two-part political system. His views as
a Federalist were at odds with Thomas Jefferson, who led the
Democratic-Republican party.

In 1794 Hamilton joined George Washington in Pennsylvania
to suppress the Whiskey Rebellion. This was the first defense
of the U.S. Constitution.

In 1797 Hamilton was accused of mishandling federal funds, but proved his innocence by publishing an embarrassing pamphlet entitled *Observations on Certain Documents*, in which he denied the charges of corruption but admitted to his scandalous relationship with Maria Reynolds.

Hamilton established the *New-York Evening Post*. One of the oldest newspapers in America, it was first published in 1801.

In 1801 Hamilton's son Philip was killed in a duel with George
Eacker, a supporter of Aaron Burr. Philip was defending his
father's honor against critical statements that had been made
by Eacker during a speech.

In 1804 Hamilton and the Federalists opposed Aaron Burr's attempt to become governor of New York. Years earlier they supported Thomas Jefferson over Burr as a candidate for the U.S. presidency.

After reading remarks that Hamilton reportedly made against him, Aaron Burr felt insulted and requested clarification and an apology. In a series of letters between the two that followed, tensions escalated and Burr demanded a duel. They met in Weehawken, New Jersey on July 11, 1804. Hamilton was mortally wounded and died soon after in New York at the age of 47.

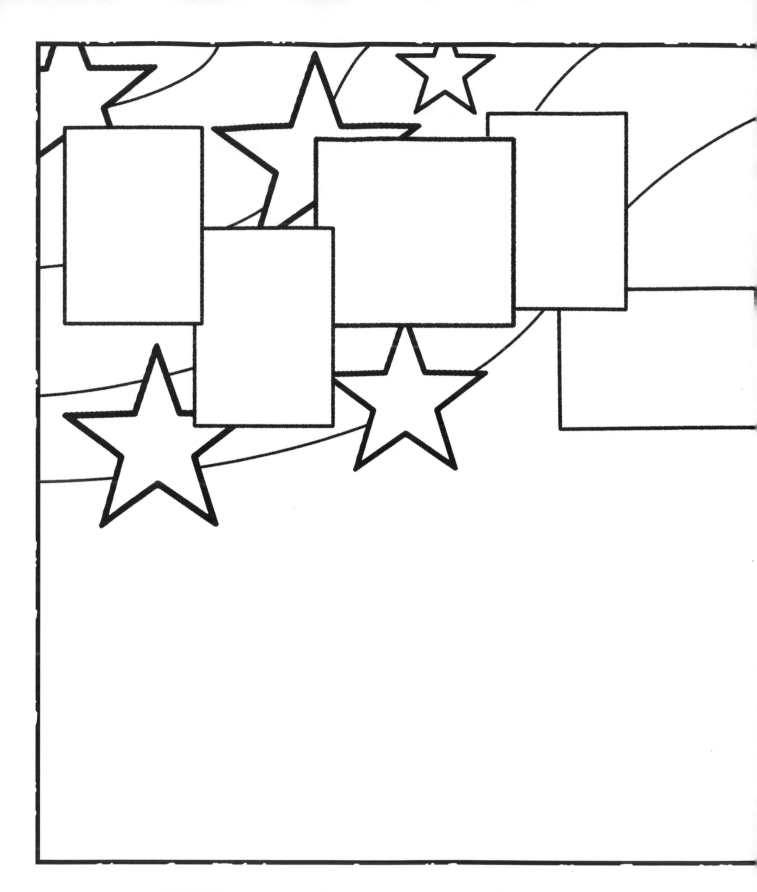

ACTIVITY: Alexander Hamilton was many things during his lifetime: author, soldier, lawyer, family man, and founding father. Use pictures or words to create a timeline of his major accomplishments.

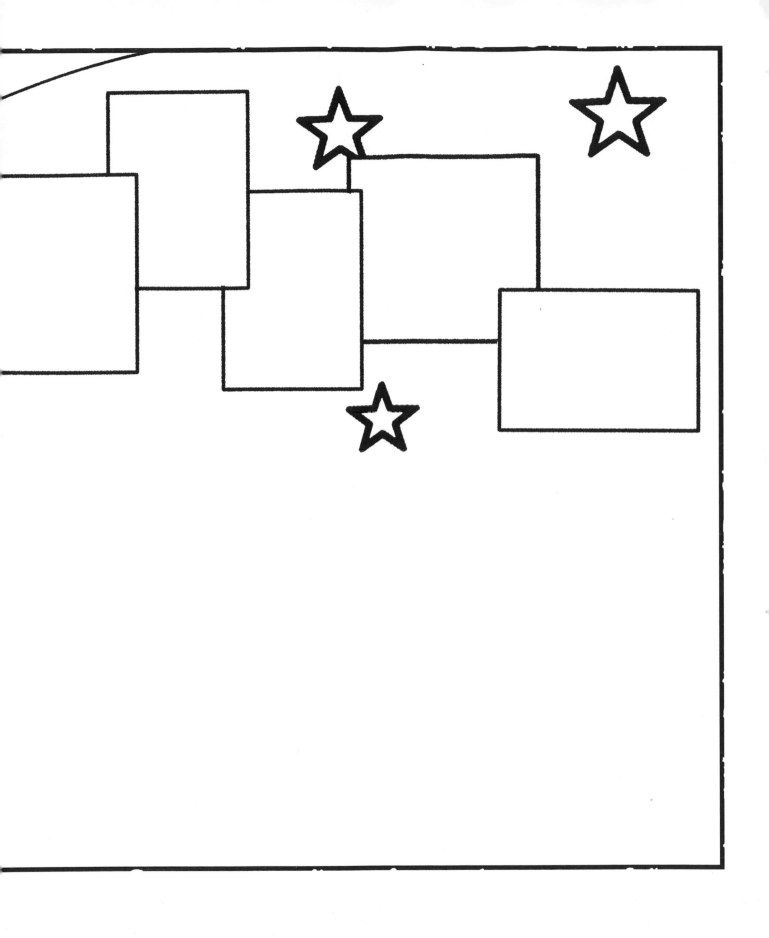